Family Treasures

Family Treasures

A Guide to Writing Your Life Stories

Margaret Mayo Gibson, Ed. D.

E-BookTime, LLC
Montgomery, Alabama

Family Treasures
A Guide to Writing Your Life Stories

Library of Congress Control Number: 2009905151

ISBN: 978-1-60862-044-9

First Edition
Published June 2009
E-BookTime, LLC
6598 Pumpkin Road
Montgomery, AL 36108
www.e-booktime.com

FAMILY TREASURES

A Guide to Writing Your Life Stories

Family Treasures are expressions of love which family and friends have for each other.

On the book cover are photographs of a grandfather's clock, a mortar and pestle, and an owl. The stories of these treasures were told at length in my first book, *A Seed in Good Soil*. Here is their meaning, briefly:

The grandfather's clock was purchased by my father as a surprise for my mother, the year I was born. It was their first piece of furniture. It stands in my living room today.

I inherited the mortar and pestle when my father died. Dad was a pharmacist and the mortar and pestle was on display in his office at Temple University Hospital.

The owl is the mascot for Temple University. Ever since my husband Tom and I met there, we have been collecting owls. The owl pictured on the cover is a memento of a trip Tom and I took to California for his 50th birthday in 1977.

A Life in Review

Memories by Theme

Memories and Beyond

ACKNOWLEDGEMENTS

With deep appreciation I thank
Family members, for their encouragement and support
Thomas Gibson
Jeffrey, Donna, Gregory, Brad Gibson
Karen, John, Jenny, John T. Dickinson

Advisory group, for their wisdom
June Bryant
Karen Dickinson
Karen Goren
Mary Smith

The book cover was designed by
John T. Dickinson

Technical assistance was provided by
Greg Gibson

My life has been blessed with family and friends who helped me grow spiritually and intellectually: my parents and grandparents, my sister Carol and my brother Bob, friends from elementary school, high school and college, friends from church and from my neighborhood, including the most recent friend, Barbara McFadden.

All scripture citations were taken from the
New International Version of the Holy Bible

PROLOGUE

WHY WRITE MEMORIES?

Writing your life stories differs from writing an autobiography. An autobiography is a history of your life. It includes dates, names and places, where events occurred. My autobiography would say, "I attended elementary school in South Philadelphia from kindergarten through sixth grade, from 1936 to 1942."

In a memoir, writing your life stories recalls your life experiences and your feelings. My memoir would say, "In my elementary school, the teacher used a ruler to rap the knuckles of any student who talked out of turn. I promised myself that if I ever became a teacher I would never do that."

We share memories so we may fully understand ourselves and to help others understand us.

When I teach classes in writing memories, people say, "I am all fired up in class. Then I get home and lose my motivation to continue writing." As a response to this, here is a guide to motivate people to write their memories when they are at home!

Why record your memories? Through your memories, people will always be able to see who you really are. Memories demonstrate your traditions and your values. Your experiences show how you faced life's obstacles and how you overcame them. Remember that you have a place in this world that nobody else has.

INTRODUCTION

HOW TO USE THIS BOOK

This is a series of the author's personal stories to stimulate your memory and help you recall details of your life experiences.

Describe your stories in your own way, with the sights, sounds, and smells, of the memories you have carried with you during your lifetime.

After you have written your own memories, refer to the chapter on Sharing Your Legacy to decide how you will preserve your memories for future generations. Read *Family Treasures* to motivate you to start writing now!

> *There is a time for everything, and a season for every activity under heaven, a time to be silent and a time to speak.* **Ecclesiastes 3:1, 3:7**

Now is the time to speak!

My Life in Review

This is a warm up. Start thinking about your life!

CHILDHOOD

My generation relied on home remedies. The grocery store and pharmacy supplied our needs: vinegar, salt, peroxide, Vicks vapor rub, castor oil, Vaseline, iodine, and baking soda (which we used for everything from indigestion and sting bites to shining the silver).

Our mass media was the radio. On Sunday, December 7, 1941, we put the radio on, as was our custom. Suddenly, we heard that the Japanese attacked Pearl Harbor. World War II had begun. Later, in a radio address, President Franklin Delano Roosevelt said, "We have nothing to fear but fear itself!" I didn't know what that meant but it sounded reassuring.

At the movie theatres, newsreels of the war were shown before the features began. They were scary but since the battles were fought so far away, the war did not seem real, until someone I knew died. Jim was 23 and had recently married my Aunt Mary's best friend. He was on a ship on the Pacific Ocean. The ship was torpedoed. Jim survived the explosion but died of drowning because there were not enough life boats. Although I was only ten years old at the time, I have been anti-war ever since.

Something else made an impression, this time a good one. It was the music of the era, music that today is still hum-able, sing-able and dance-able. With soldiers and sailors thousands of miles away, we sang, "I'll be Seeing You" and "Don't Sit Under the Apple Tree."

In the *Senior Years* chapter you can read about a person very much affected by World War II songs.

Your Life in Review

Childhood Days

When you think of the adults who raised you, what memories come to mind?

The women were...

_____

_____

The men were...

_____

_____

What do you remember about elementary school teachers and classmates?

_____

_____

How were holidays celebrated when you were a child?

_____

_____

What was your favorite food at that time?

_____

What were your favorite outdoor and indoor activities?

_____

_____

TEEN YEARS

Going to an all girls' high school limited my social life. One of my friends had an older brother, whose friends became potential dates. One of those dates took me to my senior prom. My friend and I were allowed to attend dances at the YMCA. That was pretty much the extent of my social life. Scholastically, there were courses I wanted to take but they were not offered (Italian and typing). Writing continued to be the only discipline I enjoyed.

The Good ~
Because I had been "skipped" in the elementary grades…and because I did not have an affinity for Math, it was very difficult for me, until I met Miss Clark. She was a ninth grade Algebra teacher who tutored me on her own time until I understood basics and Algebra.

And the Bad~
I was recommended for a special creative writing course. I was ecstatic until the first class. When we were seated, the teacher said, "You have 20 minutes to write an essay. You are here because you are supposed to be creative. Create!"

I promised myself that if I ever became a teacher I would have the teaching style of Miss Clark and I would help students who needed it. I would also try to motivate students to write by reading poetry and encouraging them to share their experiences and feelings.

Our high school motto "What is past is prologue." was true for me. As a whole, the education I received at the Philadelphia High School for Girls prepared me to be a lifelong learner.

Describe your social life as a teenager. Would you consider yourself shy or outgoing at this time? How important was school during your teen years?

_____

_____

_____

_____

_____

What were the good and the bad parts of being a teenager for you?

_____

_____

_____

What were your favorite subjects in high school?

_____

_____

_____

What role did extracurricular activities play during your teen years?

_____

_____

_____

_____

ADULTHOOD

College was stimulating. Although commuting precluded my being on campus very late, I joined several organizations to meet other students and to contribute to the university community. I served as president of a sorority, president of the Pan Hellenic Association and was elected to an honorary society.

After graduation I taught first at a YMCA, then at an elementary school. After I got married, I was living far from home, which necessitated making new friends and learning to be independent. My husband was at an office all day and meetings at night.

After graduating from high school, did you attend another school? If so, describe the school and the program. Did you work part time or full time? If so, describe the workplace and your responsibility.

_____

_____

_____

_____

_____

_____

_____

_____

_____

_____

_____

_____

_____

_____

_____

_____

_____

_____

_____

_____

Memories by Theme

FAITH

Grandson Greg, 4 and Granddaughter Jenny, 5 prepare to reenact the Christmas Story in 1989

Unless you change and become like little children, you will never enter the kingdom of heaven. **Matthew 18:3**

Death and Eternal Life

My mother, my daughter Karen, and I visited the cemetery one month after my father died. At Dad's grave, my mother cried, "Grandpop is celebrating his birthday in the dirt!" Five year old Karen replied, "He's not in the dirt, Grandmom. He's in heaven with Jesus!"

Karen had accepted the explanation of Jesus' life as it was told to her and she offered it to her grandmother at a time when her grandmother needed the reminder.

A Major Decision

After 28 years with the Boy Scouts of America, Tom decided to resign. The national office was moving to Texas and the family situation was not conducive to our moving that far from New Jersey. Tom had never worked for anyone else and, at age 52, it didn't look easy to get another job! Our children were in college, I was pursuing an advanced degree and Tom needed to find work right after the Scouts left. He took the first job he could find.

"How is everything at work?" I asked. "It is a job," he answered. "I can't be out of work so I will stay there. I must commute to Manhattan. I am probably lucky to get what I did." I prayed for Tom to get another job. One day Tom attended a luncheon. During table conversation Tom found out about a job opening at the national office of the Leukemia Society of America and he decided to check it out. During a lunch break that same week, Tom went for an interview and got the job. He worked for the Society for 14 years until he retired.

If you have faith as small as a mustard seed, you can say to this mountain, "Move from here to there" and it will move. Nothing will be impossible for you. **Matthew 17:20**

Describe a time when you received an answer to a prayer.

_____

_____

_____

_____

_____

_____

_____

_____

_____

Tell about a time when you did not receive the answer to a prayer that you hoped for. What was the outcome? How did you cope? Looking back, how do you feel about the way that things worked out?

_____

_____

_____

_____

_____

_____

_____

_____

_____

_____

God's Message

At 15, Grandson John T. wrote this confirmation essay:

"I think God speaks to people through music. I think I help other people hear God's message when I play the trumpet and the drums. God gave me this gift to use.

Sometimes things happen that make me feel like someone is watching over us. When it's a sunny day, I feel someone is there. I also believe God speaks through people, especially the people who don't have the best lives but are still happy. They make me feel better just seeing them and talking with them.

I believe there is a God who watches over us and speaks to us through many different ways, to let us know never to give up and that there is always someone who loves us. I think God helps me when I'm nervous and scared because, no matter what happens, I'll still be loved and He will love me even if I mess up. Church has helped me realize this."

Read more about Johnny's gifts in the chapter, *Talents*.

John T., his favorite pastime, now his career.

What gifts have you been given? Name the kind of gifts: Arts and Crafts, Sports, Academics, Music, Writing, Painting or Leadership. How have you been able to share those gifts to help others?

Read even more about gifts in the chapter, *Talents*.

Brad and the Tsunami

Grandson Brad, when he was 14 years old, wrote a reaction to the Tsunami disaster in 2002.

"I believe the question is not why God let this happen, but how can I value my life and the lives of others? We should not try to make distinctions between people who live in Asia and those who live in America, just as the waves move according to gravity, rather than the will of a vengeful judge. As far as God allowing suffering, I believe the greatest strength of humans is the ability to feel, even if the feeling is pain. Therefore, God allows suffering, but also allows for good deeds that follow."

What was the worst natural disaster in your memory? How were you affected?

_____

_____

_____

_____

_____

_____

_____

_____

_____

What other hardship have you had to face? How did you overcome it?

_____

_____

_____

_____

_____

_____

_____

_____

_____

_____

_____

Safe Passage

The morning of October 10, 1991 was very foggy in Southeastern Pennsylvania but I had to drive to work. I was a newly hired college professor. At age sixty, I needed to prove to myself that the years of financial and physical strain to earn a doctor's degree were not in vain. To reduce the stress of a daily four hour commute I spent a few nights weekly at my daughter's home.

When the fog intensified, my daughter suggested, "You can make the trip shorter. Turn right at the end of our development. About ¼ mile away is a left turn onto a highway that goes straight to the college."

Visibility was poor but I found the left turn onto the highway. I had gone about 20 yards when I saw headlights coming straight towards me. I was on the wrong side of the road! Soon I saw the outline of a truck. My heart was pounding so loudly my ears hurt. I screamed, "Dear Jesus, help me!"

I felt the car going backward, quickly. I held on to the steering wheel, not steering, just holding on, as tightly as I could. Finally, the car stopped. I was at the left turn that led to the highway. My heart was still racing. In a few seconds the truck rumbled by. I held my breath as I saw the card I kept on the dashboard: *Those who hope in the Lord will renew their strength. They will soar on wings like eagles.* Isaiah 40:31

Have you ever had an extraordinary experience? If so, describe it.

_____

_____

_____

_____

_____

_____

What role does faith play in your life when you have success and joy?

_____

_____

_____

_____

_____

_____

How has faith helped you in times of trouble?

_____

_____

_____

_____

_____

_____

Granddaughter Jenny's Confirmation Essay

I think my faith in God is like my relationship with my friends. They talk to me and show what is right, just like God would do. So far my faith in God has shown that I've gone to church and have been around the people that mean the most to me and have done the things I have wanted. By God being there and loving me, he made all these things possible. Just like dancing and singing in the church choir, I show how I feel about God by expressing myself through the things I love best. When I see my friends in church and out of church I see God and the work of God because God made each and every one of us and showed that each of us was made differently.

When I look for faith, trust, and support to find God I look in my heart and in my friends' hearts. My friends are a huge part of my faith journey. They'll always be. Jesus influences me the same as God does. God created all things in this world and made his son Jesus to interact with them. Jesus is my most important friend because he listens, watches and cares for me. Most of all I know he loves me.

Granddaughter Jenny, best friend Mandy Flathmann, a special day with Grandmom Margie, 1995

How did friends support you during your teen years? Who has remained your friend in adulthood?

_____

_____

_____

_____

_____

_____

Describe a friend from childhood. Tell about an experience that the two of you shared.

_____

_____

_____

_____

_____

In what ways are your friends precious to you now?

_____

_____

_____

_____

_____

A friend loved at all times. **Proverbs 17:17**

FAMILY

**Great Grandmom Jenny Borrelli Pistoia with
Great Grandson Jeffrey Gibson, Mom Margie Gibson,
Grandmom Margaret Mayo, 1955**

**Grandpop Tom Gibson with Granddaughter
Jennifer Dickinson, Great Grandmom Ruth Gibson,
Mom Karen Dickinson 1985**

*"How neat it would be to be one gentle spirit and still lose
none of the cultural traditions and family way of life that
we knew."* **Jeffrey Gibson 2007**

My Mother, Margaret Borrelli Mayo

Mom was a great Italian cook. The aroma of Mom's homemade Italian meatballs, lentil soup, ravioli, and cream puffs was enough to send me scurrying to the dinner table.

Mom was thrifty. She made meals from pasta and beans and omelets with spinach, zucchini, or asparagus. She once commented, "All my life I dreamed of eating a steak. Now I can afford it, the doctor says that it isn't good for me!"

Mom was a migrant worker as a child. She showed me where she and her brothers and sisters waited for the wagon to take them to the farms in New Jersey. As a young adult she worked long hours in a shirt factory so Dad could go to college. After school I came home to music. The radio was playing and Mom was singing. She knew all the words to the popular songs. Today, I can't remember where I am supposed to be without consulting my calendar, but I can sing with tapes of Frank Sinatra, Bing Crosby, and Mom's favorite, Perry Como.

Mom raised us on quotations... "If you get into trouble at school you will get into double trouble at home!" "If you can't say anything nice about somebody, don't say anything at all!"

After repeating some of my mother's sayings one day, my nine year old granddaughter asked, "How many sayings did great grandmom have?" Six year old grandson Brad answered, "An infinity!" "What does that mean?" asked Jenny. "It never ends!" said Brad. It did seem that way. It was how my mother and her mother were raised. They were not formally educated but they were taught family values through the "sayings" and passed them along to me, my sister, and my brother.

My Father, Carl Mayo

Dad was a pharmacist who loved poetry. The books he owned varied from *Materia Medica* to poetry by Robert Frost. Dad's favorite pastime was doing crossword puzzles. I thought Dad was the smartest person in the world, but he would sometimes say to me when I asked for help, "There is the dictionary. Look it up." He wanted me to figure things out for myself!

When dad became a hospital pharmacist, people paid him directly. Mom told me Dad often charged people much less when he realized they were not covered by insurance. He paid the difference although he and my mother struggled financially themselves. However, I had the emotional and spiritual guidance I needed to keep a strong faith.

When I was a senior in high school Dad explained that I could go to Temple University with free tuition because he worked there full time but I would have to commute. I was not happy. I said, "I just spent four years of high school commuting by trolley and subway to an academic high school you wanted me to attend. If I cannot live on a campus, I want to work to have some spending money."

The following day Dad had some news. "I got you a job in the registrar's office at Temple University. You can start the day after graduation." I did. By March I was ready to enroll! I started courses in the fall semester and became a life long student. I retired 47 years later, as a faculty member in a university.

Dad imagined correctly that the college atmosphere would be appealing to me! Physical punishment was common in Dad's childhood but his parenting style was nurturing. I emulated that style with my children and grandchildren.

My Baby Brother Grows Up

My brother Bob is eight years younger than I and has always been a delight to me. In the last several years, he has become more than a delight. He is a comfort, an encourager, and a friend.

Through his adult years Bob lived in the same neighborhood as my parents. He was my connection to Mom and Dad. When our father died, Bob helped our mother through the grieving period as well as taking care of the legal matters. When our mother died, he provided comfort for me. Bob, his wife Joan, and his children and grand-children, are a source of joy to me and my family.

Describe the family members you recall most vividly. How do you feel about them today?

_____

_____

_____

_____

_____

_____

_____

_____

_____

Describe two memories of family times you shared.

_____

_____

_____

_____

_____

_____

_____

_____

_____

_____

HOUSES

Tom and I lived in this North Brunswick, New Jersey home 33 years. We raised our two children here.

Unless the Lord builds the house, its builders labor in vain. **Psalm 127:1**

The Row House in South Philadelphia

"Don't move off the steps," my mother warned. "I'll leave the front door open so I can hear you if you need me." My sister and I settled on the marble front steps to sleep. The first house I lived in…on Daly Street in South Philadelphia…was a row house, stifling in the summer. The fan mom bought blew hot air in our faces so, on many hot nights, we slept outside on the cool marble steps. The house was on a street wide enough for one car. In the 1930's, when I was a child, no one had a car, so the street was safe for tag and jump rope. The steps were wide enough to play jacks.

My bedroom was 9'x12'. My sister and I shared a bed, bigger than a twin size but smaller than a double bed. We had a cardboard chest for clothes that could be folded. We hung our dresses on nails behind the room door. That house held memories of homemade pasta, radio comedy, and the player piano. My grandmother owned the house and we rented it. When I was 19, our family moved into our own home in the Mount Airy section of Philadelphia. I lived there only 3 years before I married, but it was great for my mom to finally live in a house she could call her own.

Describe the house you lived in as a child. Where was it? Did you have a room of your own? Who lived there with you?

_____

_____

_____

_____

_____

_____

_____

_____

Describe a special event that occurred in that house.

_____

_____

_____

_____

_____

_____

_____

_____

_____

_____

A Second Childhood Home

When does a house become a home? It was never my formal address but I chose to spend so many hours and days there that my grandmother's house at 1934 South Juniper Street became a second home during my childhood and teen years. It was a refuge and my grandmother was my mentor. She was my counselor, my family historian, my cooking coach, and my gardening teacher. She grew herbs and flowers in clay pots and even an imported fig tree, which grew to be as high as her second story. Her home was a welcome stop for my friends and a haven for me.

The journey to Juniper Street started when I was born. My grandmother, a widow at 36, had remarried at 40. She became pregnant the same time as my mother, who had been married for four years. At delivery, I was small but healthy. My grandmother's baby was stillborn. My mother began taking me to my grand-mother's house to be company for her. At 8, I was considered old enough to go by myself.

In the summertime, I packed a large cardboard box with clothes to last a few days, and walked the 7 blocks. I still remember the jeers from neighborhood children laughing at my "suitcase". At Grandmom's house I had attention, praise and encouragement, and, my own bedroom! I was blessed to have Grandmom at my college graduation and my wedding. She gave me a surprise bridal shower. I was thrilled to do the same for my granddaughter!

Were you ever welcomed into someone else's house so that you felt it was your second home? Describe the relationship. Was it a relative or friend? Why did you feel so welcome?

_____

_____

_____

_____

_____

_____

_____

_____

_____

_____

_____

_____

_____

_____

_____

_____

_____

_____

_____

_____

The Love Nest

"We have an apartment," said my fiancé. "I hope you like it. The location is excellent. I believe we can make it look darn cute. The monthly rent is $50 plus electricity."

I traveled to Altoona from Philadelphia to see what Tom had found. I was happy with it because it meant we were to be together. When my mom came to see it she said, "My goodness, you will be living in an attic!" Tom said, "I think of it as a love nest. We are two love birds!"

Yes, it was a converted attic. There was a small living room that opened into the bedroom, a kitchen small enough to reach the refrigerator from the drop-leaf table where we ate. The bathroom ceiling was too low for a man to stand up straight to use the toilet. It was our first home. Our son was born there. After fifty five years no place touches my heart like the love nest.

**Margie poses outside our love nest, our home in
Altoona, Pennsylvania, 1953-1955.**

Describe the first place you lived after you left home...

_____

_____

_____

_____

_____

_____

_____

_____

_____

Who else lived in that house? What was the relationship to you? How long did you live there?

_____

_____

_____

_____

_____

_____

_____

_____

_____

_____

_____

When Memories of a Place Are Sad

My two year old son Jeff and I tapped several times on the outside window of the living room in the first floor apartment. Finally, Betty, eight months pregnant, appeared at the window and motioned for us to leave.

"Jeff and I are ready to go shopping with you," I reminded her. Betty refused to open the window and motioned for us to go away. "What is wrong?" I asked, "Are you ok?" Betty shook her head no. Through the window, she said, "I have a terrible cold. I don't want Jeff to get whatever I have."

Betty had a car. I did not. She was generous in transporting Jeff and me to shop and sightsee. Betty and I were living far from our families and our husbands traveled. We had become friends. She adored Jeff. Now she was anxious and shouted, "Take Jeff away before he gets my germs!"

When we returned to our apartment, Betty called. "I am so sorry I acted rude," she said. "I don't want Jeff to catch whatever I have. My husband is coming home to take me to the doctor. I need something to protect the baby. I'll speak with you tomorrow."

The next morning Betty's husband called to say that Betty was in the hospital with meningitis. The doctor had delivered the baby and Betty was in a coma. The baby was fine. Three weeks later Betty died. Forty five years later, I visited the apartment complex in Virginia, where I knew Betty. I stood in front of the window where I had last seen Betty. I thanked God for her friendship and her protection of our two year old son.

There are memories in every house or apartment where you lived. Sad memories are also a part of your history.

Can you remember a sad time in a place where you lived? How can sad memories help you?

_____

_____

_____

_____

_____

_____

_____

_____

_____

_____

_____

_____

_____

_____

_____

_____

_____

_____

Every experience is a part of who we are today. All of our memories, including the sad ones, can leave us stronger and wiser...and at peace.

The First Family Residence

My husband was transferred to the National Headquarters of the Boy Scouts of America, in North Brunswick, New Jersey, in 1959. After two years in an apartment we moved to our first home. Our daughter Karen was born in 1960. We lived there for the next 32 years. We raised children, volunteered at our church, held family gatherings, and made new friends. Tom held several communications positions at the Boy Scouts of America. Later, Tom worked for the Leukemia Society as Vice President of Communications for the Leukemia Society. When the children started school I taught in the local elementary school, got a master's degree in counseling, and eventually, after receiving a doctorate, I taught at Rutgers University.

"You never leave a place you love. You go away taking part of it along, leaving part of you remaining."
Anonymous

Describe the house where you lived the longest time.

_____

_____

_____

_____

_____

_____

_____

_____

_____

_____

In which house do you hold the fondest memories? Describe some of those memories.

_____

_____

_____

_____

_____

_____

_____

_____

_____

_____

Retirement Houses

In 1992, when Tom retired, we moved to Glen Mills, PA to be near our children and grandchildren. Tom stayed busy as a volunteer in several organizations, including Rotary International, and the local American Legion post. He became an active church volunteer and successfully continued writing newsletters and columns, as a volunteer. I started a new career as a member of the faculty at West Chester University. My fondest memory of the townhouse was having our grandchildren stay overnight.

Re-fired, not Re-tired!

Twelve years later, with increased physical problems like backaches and stiff knees, we moved to a one floor house in an active 55+ community in Concord Township, PA. When my daughter heard about our busy schedule she decided we were re-fired, not re-tired!

Activities, fitness opportunities, and new social contacts, are leading to more memories. My next door neighbor held a book signing on the publication of my first book.

What memories do you hold for the house you are living in now?

_____

_____

_____

_____

_____

_____

_____

_____

_____

_____

What was your favorite house? Why? Describe the house and some memories of the time you lived there.

_____

_____

_____

_____

_____

_____

_____

_____

_____

_____

What does retirement mean to you?
~being able to relax
~pursuing a hobby
~doing volunteer work
~spending more time with family
~getting a part time job
~joining organizations
~traveling
~watching television

Perhaps retirement means to you some of the above, all of the above, or none of the above!

Describe what retirement means to you and where those goals fit into your life now.

_____

_____

_____

_____

_____

_____

_____

_____

_____

_____

_____

_____

_____

LOVE

**Margaret and Carl Mayo, in 1961,
on their 34th wedding anniversary**

Tom and Margie Gibson wed, April 11, 1953

*And now these three remain: faith, hope, and love. But
the greatest of these is love.* **I Corinthians 13:13**

Carl and Margaret…
Without Approval

It was 1923, at the Italian Market in South Philadelphia. Two women approached each other and exclaimed, "Giovanna!" "Carolina!" After 33 years, my mother's mother and my father's mother, who had been neighbors in Italy, discovered they were neighbors in America.

Giovanna Borrelli invited Carolina Malamisuro to her home for ice cream and cake. Carolina brought her oldest child, 16 year old Carl. Giovanna asked her oldest child, 16 year old Margaret, to serve in the parlor. When Margaret reached Carl, she looked at him, got flustered and spilled the ice cream all over Carl's lap. It was love at first spill!

Carolina told my dad, "Do not get serious about Margaret." But the teenagers fell in love and four years later, on July 11, 1927, Carl faced an enraged mother. "I told you to stop seeing Margaret!" she shouted. "We did not come to America so you could marry poor. I forbid you to ever see Margaret again!"

Carl ran to Margaret's house. "We are leaving," he said. "We are getting married." They took a train to Media and got married by a Justice of the Peace. They lived with Giovanna, my mother's mother.

In 2001, 100 years after my grandparents immigrated to America, my husband and I took a trip to the village in Southern Italy where both sets of grandparents were born. The village had been founded in 720 A.D. By the 19th century the land was depleted. I understood why our grandparents immigrated to the United States. I understood why my father's parents wanted a better life for my father, their oldest child. I didn't understand why they tried to keep my parents apart when they were so much in love.

If you have any negative memories about a relationship, you can write them down and release them. You can forgive and let go because the power that person held in your memory bank is now gone.

_____

_____

_____

_____

_____

_____

What is the history of your parents' marriage? How did they meet? Did they have the consent of your grandparents?

_____

_____

_____

_____

_____

What influence did your parents have on you? What traditions do you keep? What do you do differently?

_____

_____

_____

_____

_____

Tom and Margie
Fated to be Mated!

"He is an outstanding senior!" said Freddy. I looked skeptically at the fellow who was trying to convince me to date someone I did not know. "If he is outstanding, how come I never heard of him?" Apparently, Tom Gibson had seen me around campus and asked Freddy for my phone number. I needed to check this out. I asked some classmates who said they knew who Tom was. They thought he was really nice.

At age 20 I still did not have permission to go on a blind date. I obeyed my parents! My parents were not comfortable with my dating a veteran, even if the veteran was a college student. It meant that the man was at least four years older than I. Because Freddy agreed to accompany Tom to my house and "properly" introduce us, my mother finally relented. Tom had asked me to go to a picnic, sponsored by Alpha Phi Omega, a Boy Scout fraternity. My mother insisted that I dress like a lady and wear a skirt. It took some convincing to allow me to wear slacks to a picnic!

That evening I was dressing for the picnic when my mother came into my room to tell me there were two young men downstairs. She said, "One is dressed like a gentleman, one is dressed like a hobo. You had better be going out with the one who is dressed like a gentleman." "What is the gentleman wearing?" I asked. "A tuxedo," mom answered. "Mother, if someone is wearing a tuxedo to go to a picnic, he is nuts! What is the other man wearing?" "He is wearing dungarees." "That's more appropriate," I sighed. I went downstairs. Freddy introduced Tom to me and to my mother, then left to go to a prom.

Tom and I took a bus to the picnic. If anyone ever asks about love at first sight, I can truthfully say I believe it. It happened to me!

Tom and I came from different cultural backgrounds. When I first met his mother, she said, "I never thought my son would marry a foreigner." I was confused. My dad was born in Clairton, PA and my mom was born in Winsted, Connecticut. As far as I knew those two towns were in the USA. Later, I realized that it was my Italian heritage which made Tom's mother uncomfortable. I went home and told my mother I could never marry Tom. "You are not marrying his mother. Remember the story of my mother-in-law," she reminded me. After Tom and I married, Tom's mother became a devoted mother-in-law and grandmother. Before she died, she said I was the best daughter-in-law, wife, and mother, anybody could have. Thanks be to God!

We met just a few weeks before Tom graduated college and in the next two years, before we wed, he was in Altoona, PA and I was in Philadelphia. From the time we started to date until the years after we married, when he traveled for his work, Tom wrote many letters to me. He kept me up to date with his job and life in the working world. His letters were very dear to me, as we pursued our long distance romance. Here are excerpts from letters that touch my heart, fifty six years later.

Before We Were Married...

February, 1952
"On the traditional sweetheart's day, think of me and know that I am longing for you and loving you as best I can from 250 miles away!"

March, 1952
"If I showed good taste in choosing your necklace, then surely I've displayed much better taste in choosing you as my life's companion. I love you and I melt just looking at you. When I hold you I realize what a wonderful girl is now part of my life."

December, 1952
"I find myself wondering how I ever got someone as fine and nice as you!"

After We Were Married...

March 1963, from San Diego, California
"Good to hear that I'm missed by you and the kids. So are you and the kids! LUV, GIB"

October, 1963, from Tulsa, Oklahoma
"I've missed my fine family and beautiful wife-and will be looking forward to seeing you all on Sunday. Luv you. As ever, Gib"

April, 1964, from St. Petersburg, Florida,
"Tomorrow I have an interview at Cape Kennedy with the man who instructs astronauts. It should be interesting! Luv you, as ever, Gib"

Describe the relationship between you and someone you love deeply. Where did you meet? Do you have any letters or cards you kept as mementoes of your courtship?

_____

_____

_____

_____

_____

_____

_____

_____

_____

_____

What were the obstacles to your romance?

_____

_____

_____

_____

_____

_____

_____

_____

_____

_____

MEMORABLE PERSONS

Peggy, brother Bob, and sister Carol, 1984

I will not forget you. **Isaiah 49:15**

My Sister Carol

Carol and I were only ten and a half months apart but we looked very different. She was born with blue eyes and blond curly hair. I had dark brown eyes and straight brown hair. Carol was tall and large-boned. I was short and small-boned. Her doctor was not convinced we were related. He said to me, "You don't have to say you are sisters to visit Carol in the hospital, just say you are friends." I protested, "I AM her sister!" He replied, "Okay, say you are good friends!" We started as sisters. We became friends.

Carol had many physical problems. As a child she had pneumonia at three months and kidney dysfunction when she was ten years old. As an adult she had diabetes and heart trouble. When her cardiologist told her she should have died years earlier, she changed doctors!

My sister Carol had the soul of a poet and an indomitable spirit. With a social worker, she co-led support groups at the nursing home where she resided her last few years. Carol gave me unconditional love. She shared joy at my successes and sympathized with my sorrows. Today, her son Carl and his wife Michelle continue that legacy. Throughout her life, Carol wrote poetry. The following three poems are from a collection written shortly before she died.

Pride

It makes you laugh, it makes you cry.
It makes you hold your head up high.
"A haughty being, she, I vow" is heard as you pass by.
It's good, it's bad, who can say.
Which side you're on will pave the way.
Until all people will agree, I will walk with head held high,
Surveying my kingdom from the throne
As I kiss the world goodbye.

The Angels Cry

A man is murdered, a wife is beaten.
Children on the street have hardly eaten.
A man leaves a bar, an accident in a car.
A skid on a pavement, a woman slid too far.
A plane crashes, explodes in mid-air.
People turn to ashes, oh so hard to bear.
The grief went to the heavens. It spread so far and wide.
God looked down on earth, and the angels cried.

God's Labor

The sun is shining bright as can be, the flowers are blooming pink
    and white.
I stand up here among the clouds and take in the gorgeous sight.
The day is God's gift of beauty, to all who will partake.
Who will stop and smell the roses and praise the scene that God
    makes?
My soul is singing, my burden will not start.
I thank you Lord, for this day, from the bottom of my heart.

Tell about a memorable person in your life.

_____

_____

_____

_____

_____

_____

_____

Who built up your confidence when you were growing up?

_____

_____

_____

_____

_____

_____

Who inspired you to reach your goals? Who were your mentors?

_____

_____

_____

_____

_____

_____

NAMES

**Aunt Serafina (Sadie), Michela-Margaret), Grandmom
Giovanna (Jenny), Margie's college graduation from
Temple University, 1952**

*A good name is more desirable than great riches; to be
esteemed is better than silver or gold.* **Proverbs 22:1**

Peggy/Margie

My mother was born in Winsted, Connecticut where her father worked in a watch factory. When the factory closed, the family returned to Italy where my grandparents were born. Five years later, they immigrated again to the USA. At Ellis Island the customs officer asked my mother's name. My grandmother answered, "Michela". "That is Michael, a boy's name," the officer said, "her name is Margaret."

When I was born my dad wanted me named for my mother. She was Margaret. I am Margaret. I never thought the name suited me. My family and childhood friends still call me Peggy. I thought Margie sounded cuter so I introduced myself to Tom as "Margie". Friends after 1953 call me Margie. My sister in law Joan calls me Peggy/ Margie!

When my brother was two years old, Dad changed our last name legally. The Malamisuro family became the Mayo family. When the Sons of Italy announced the change in their newspaper, it was spelled, "Meo". Dad showed me the paper. "Don't Italians know how to spell?" I asked. Dad, always the teacher, explained. In Italian, there is no "y" and "e" says "a". The teachable moment worked. I have always remembered that. Mayo sounds like Meo in Italian.

My husband was named for his father, Thomas Mc Clay Gibson, who did not want his son to be called "Junior". Henceforth my father-in-law was called Mc Clay and my husband, Thomas. Each of our two children chose Thomas as a middle name for one son.

Why was your first name chosen?

_____

_____

_____

Do you have any nicknames or pet names?

_____

_____

_____

How do you feel about your name?

_____

_____

_____

What would you name someone? Why?

_____

_____

_____

What is the origin of your last name?

_____

_____

_____

_____

_____

PARENTING

Margie, Tom, Karen, Jeff. The four of us.

**Then there were six!
Jeff and Donna, Tom and Margie, John and Karen!**

You may give your children your love but not your thoughts, for they have their own thoughts. You may strive to be like them, but seek not to make them like you, for life goes not backward nor tarries with yesterday. You are the bows from which your children as living arrows are sent forth. **Kalil Gibran**

Chicken! Chicken! Chicken!

The summer heat wilted the flowers and turned the grass to straw. Three eleven year old boys wandered near their housing development, trying to think of something to do. One boy was our son Jeff, the other two, his neighborhood friends.

"No place to swim and too hot to play ball," said Eddie.

"Let's go find out what's inside that empty house at the end of the field," suggested Joey.

"It's probably locked up," said Jeff.

"So what, we'll break in," answered Joey.

"I'm not going," Jeff said as he started to walk home.

"Chicken! Chicken! Chicken!" Eddie and Joey yelled.

"You're home early," I said when Jeff got home.

"I just felt like coming home," Jeff said.

Two hours later, Joey's mother called me.

"Why wasn't Jeff at the police station?" she asked.

"Why would Jeff be at the police station?" I replied.

"I thought Jeff was with Joey and Eddie this afternoon. Didn't Jeff go to that vacant house with them?"

"Jeff has been home for a while. What happened?" I asked.

Joey's mother explained. "A little while ago, someone saw the boys break into the house and called the police.

The boys were taken to the police station and I got a call to go get Joey at the station. Why wasn't Jeff there?"

"I don't know," I answered and hung up.

I asked Jeff if he knew about the break in. He said, "Yeah but I knew it wasn't right so I came home, even though they yelled at me "Chicken! Chicken! Chicken!" I didn't tell you because I didn't want to squeal on my friends."

What would you have said to your child in the same situation (confronted with the decision to go along with the group to vandalize)?

_____

_____

_____

_____

_____

_____

_____

_____

I learned that children can use good judgment. They do not need never ending lectures. They need an opportunity to figure things out for themselves.

What have you learned from your children? Tell about it from an event that happened.

_____

_____

_____

_____

_____

_____

_____

_____

When Two Became Four

My husband and I are blessed to have children who married wonderful people. Our two children became four when, within eight months, our son Jeff married Donna and our daughter Karen married John.

Donna is a terrific wife to Jeff, a terrific mother to Greg and Brad and a great daughter-in-law. When husband Tom was 80, our daughter and son-in-law planned a huge party at their home for family and friends. On the actual date, we invited neighbors to our house. Because the others were working or out of town, Donna came alone, from New Jersey, bringing food and her friendly persona. She made such a hit that, at the end of the evening, people were asking me to Rent-A-Donna!

John is a project engineer, in addition to being a great husband to Karen and a great father to Jenny and Johnny. After we settled on a date to move into our new home, there were serious problems. I told the builder I would bring John to inspect the house. "He can't," said the builder. "If he is in the building business, I cannot allow it." I said, "No son-in-law, no settlement!" The builder was firm. John called the builder and talked with him. After the telephone talk, John was permitted to inspect the house. Everything was resolved and we moved in.

How have in-laws enriched your life?

GRANDPARENTING

What I Learned from My Grandchildren

Top, Brad, Greg, Grandmom Margie, John T., Jenny

Children's children are a crown to the aged, and parents are the pride of their children. **Proverbs 17:6**

Jenny

A birthday letter to me from Jenny:

What exactly is a grandmom? There are many answers to that question. A grandmom is someone that listens, talks, and is always interested in everything and anything everyone is doing (even if she doesn't know the person). If you don't have a grandmom you are missing out on one of the greatest persons that will ever be involved in your life. My grandmom:

-loves everyone
-listens to everyone
-talks to everyone
-makes everyone feel special
-reminds me how much she loves me and how proud she is of me every time she sees me.
I LOVE YOU, Nonna! Jenny

More about Jenny

"Your class pet is a rat?" I asked. "I will come to your open house but I do not want to see a rat!" I insisted.

"Grandmom, it is just a pet."

"I cannot accept a rat as a pet. Don't you remember the story of how I was frightened by rats when I was a child? I was so scared I could not sleep at night."

"I know about that," said Jenny, "but this is different. It is a cute little white rat, not a big brown one and it is in a cage. Just come to see it."

I went. When we approached the cage, Jenny took the rat out and held it. "Grandmom, you can pet the rat."

"No."

"Try."

I looked at my smiling seven year old granddaughter holding the animal. Who is the adult here, I wondered.

I reached out and touched the rat.

"See," said Jenny, "it is ok."

"Yes, it is ok. This IS different."

Describe a fond memory of yourself as a grandchild.

_____

_____

_____

_____

_____

_____

When did you learn something from a grandchild?

_____

_____

_____

_____

_____

_____

When was the last time you were with a child or a group of children? What did you learn about children or about life in general?

_____

_____

_____

_____

_____

_____

Gregory
An 8th Grade Poem

A Ride Through the Path of Choice

The breath of fall whispers as you glide along the hills.
A rummaging of emotion passes in and out.
The banks of nature are yet a single thought, as you turn the bend of
destiny.
Your thoughts are interrupted by the approach of an intersection.
The will of you cajoles to the left, while your intellect logistically
faces right.
You know now that it is time for yet another decision.
Deep inside you wish that it wasn't yours to make.

In an instant, relief of pressure is possessed
And a turn is made, toward the best.

What was the easiest decision you have had to make?

_____

_____

_____

_____

_____

_____

_____

_____

_____

_____

What was the hardest decision you have had to make?

_____

_____

_____

_____

_____

_____

_____

_____

_____

_____

Brad
Eight Years Old

"Grandmom, isn't my pool fun? I can do tricks in the water. You can too."

"No, Brad, I cannot put my head in the water."

"Sure you can."

"I almost drowned when I was a little girl. I never go in the water very far."

"It is safe here. I will show you."

Brad put his head in the water and held it there for several seconds.

"Brad. I am over 60 years old and I have never put my head in the water."

"Oh, but I will hold your hand."

Nine year old Brad stood in the shallow water, in his backyard pool, and held out his hand. I took it. I drew in a breath…and put my head in the water.

Unknown to me, my husband turned on his camera when he heard the conversation. There is a visual record of a little boy holding his grandmother's hand, while she quickly dunked her head under the water.

Has a grandchild ever encouraged you to do something?

Brad
An 8th Grade Poem

I Don't Understand

Why do so many hate?
Why do so many suffer?
Why do so many eat when many more hunger?
Why is she so sick? Why is he so poor?
Why do so many feel that they have to go to war?
There are so many things that I do not understand.
Why must my brother fight, so he can be a man?
Is there one true religion, one way to see the light?
I wish I knew the answer, so we could stop this fight.
There is one very big thing, we all must understand.
We must accept each other, or forever alone, we stand.

How do you feel when you hear of a natural disaster? What is the role of humankind?

_____

_____

_____

_____

_____

_____

_____

_____

_____

_____

_____

_____

_____

_____

_____

_____

_____

_____

_____

_____

_____

SENIOR YEARS

**Presenters daughter-in-law Donna and daughter Karen join
Margie at intermission. Women's Conference,
Reformation Lutheran Church, 2002**

*They will still bear fruit in old age. They will stay fresh
and green.* **Psalm 92:14**

Age is Just a Number!

A look at aging from grandchildren's perspectives...

Brad ...
Aging means more independence, more freedom, although it also means more responsibility, like paying bills. Old is a misused term. Although 60, 70, or 80 might seem old to some people, that's just a chronological term for a physical state. You can act old at any age. You will never get old if you are optimistic, friendly, outgoing, and open-minded!

Jenny...
Growing old is happiness! You get many experiences in your life that will come and go but growing old means you're getting the chance to experience love, hate, friends, fights, romance. Growing old should not be considered a hard time but as a time when you can look back on good memories-some may not be so good but you need the experience to find out for yourself.

Johnny...
Getting old has both good and not so good points. There are always good and bad points to everything. When you are 50, you can join the PGA tour for those over 50. That is one of the good points. As you get older your body does begin to deteriorate and of course that is one of the bad points. I guess it can get a little scary. But you can do more things that you want to do, so that is another good point.

On the Road

When I made my last visit to supervise student teachers before my retirement the principal invited me to speak at a Parent meeting in the fall. I agreed. After the presentation a parent said to me, "You were good at the DuPont Company but tonight was the best." I explained that I had never done a parenting talk at DuPont. 'Well, you should!" she replied.

The next day I called DuPont to ask about being a speaker. "We schedule speakers only through an agency," the program liaison told me. I had retired, I was almost 65, and I did not want to bother applying to an agency. My daughter asked what I was going to do next. "I looked up retirement and I do not see your name or picture!" she said. She smiled but I knew she had a point. I called the agency DuPont mentioned and the director first asked my credentials. Her second question was "How soon can you start?"

A new career began, Parenting Consultant for industry. I visited headquarters during the lunch hour when employees gathered to hear speakers. After three years, I stopped when I had to drive several miles during a blizzard. Industry does not close for bad weather the way schools do!

I continued the parenting sessions as a volunteer at local schools. When a new pastor came to our church he invited me to do a parenting series on Sundays. When I was 70 I decided that was enough. One parent said, "You must write a book. We need to know how to raise our children! Don't forget to include your childhood memories. That made the sessions interesting."

My first book was born!

Music...and its Power!

When I heard that my presentation, *Sharing Your Life Stories*, was scheduled for two hours I asked that there be a break. The activities director at the senior facility agreed. I cannot explain why, but the day before my scheduled talk, I purchased a recording of songs popular during the 1940's to use for the break. I had never played music during a break. I used the time to listen to memories people wanted to share privately with me and gave others an opportunity to share with each other.

The Andrew Sisters came on and a man asked if dancing were allowed. I said that I was sure it would be fine. He said that he was asking for his wife and then sat down. His wife got up, came to me, and proceeded to twirl me around in perfect rhythm to a Jitterbug. Everyone in the audience seemed to enjoy the spontaneous entertainment. I did too! After the session, the husband said to me, "That was wonderful. Thank you so much. My wife has Alzheimer's and has been unresponsive. This is the first time she has shown any sign of remembering anything in a long time."

I have heard that God puts you where you ought to be. That day, I really believed it.

Teach us to number our days aright, that we may gain a heart of wisdom. **Psalm 90:12**

When have you felt that you were in a place for a certain reason? Describe the circumstances.

_____

_____

_____

_____

_____

_____

_____

_____

How has music been a part of your life?

_____

_____

_____

_____

_____

_____

_____

_____

Those who hope in the Lord will renew their strength. They will soar on wings like eagles; they will run and not grow weary, they will walk and not be faint. Isaiah 40:31

TALENTS

Jenny the teacher

**John T. the trumpeter, left
Brad, the saxophonist, right**

Greg, the drummer

*To one he gave five talents, to another two talents, and to
another one talent, each according to his ability.*
Matthew 25:15

Your Best Thing

"I can't do anything right," said a student in my first grade class. "Me either," said another. Soon there was a chorus of "I can't." That evening I wrote a poem. The next day, I recited it to the class. We agreed to look for the thing each of us could do well, especially after I revealed the poem was about me!

Maggie's Gift

Once upon a time, in a place not too far,
lived a girl named Maggie, in a town called Gillar.
It was there that this story, which is really quite true,
Happened to Maggie, and is now told to you.

When Maggie was a toddler, when she was very small,
She was called "gifted" by one and by all.
Cause Maggie could remember long poems galore
And when Maggie was read to, she shouted for more!

In school the teacher told her the little word "pan"
And Maggie said, "Now I know fan, tan, and ran!"
Maggie could think of hard words and some rhymes
That no one had taught her, she was alone at those times.

As Maggie grew older, she didn't quite know
If she were still gifted, or not really so.
She fell off the ropes and the balance beam too.
All the girls laughed, honest and true!
In Math class she worried, she had trouble counting,
Each day at school, her troubles were mounting!
In Art class she fumbled with yarn and with glue.
She looked at the mess and said, "Now what'll I do?"
Penelope Prescott, well-dressed but not nice

Told Maggie to "give up" and told her it twice!
Days passed and Maggie felt very sad.
Each day at school she felt very bad.
She was finding more things that she could not do
And the list of her failures just grew and grew.
"Am I really gifted?" Maggie asked with a sigh,
How can I know what gift have I?"

"You'll know," said friend Jane, "please don't cry.
Cheer up, keep going, give words a try."

Maggie then did, what she liked to do best.
She wrote her own stories and did it with zest.
She wrote about people and animals and Spring.
She wrote about school and almost any old thing.

And then it happened, on a bright sunny day,
When Maggie was telling her stories at play
A teacher who heard her, shouted with glee,
"Why Maggie, those stories sound good to me!"

The teacher bound the stories right into a book.
To know what her gift was, Maggie just had to look.
In the book were her stories, some funny, some sad.
Story writing was her gift and Maggie was glad,

When you find something that you like to do
And you learn to do it, through, through, and through
You can feel happy and peaceful too
That you found your gift and it's part of you.
Just look around, at people near you,
And try to help them find their gifts too.

We have different gifts, according to the grace given us.
Romans 12:6

What are your gifts? How long ago did you discover what you can do well?

_____

_____

_____

_____

_____

_____

_____

_____

_____

_____

How have you used your gifts in a job or in volunteer work? How can you pass along your gifts as part of your legacy?

_____

_____

_____

_____

_____

_____

_____

_____

_____

TRAVEL

**Tom and Margie hold the Italian flag as they recall their
trip to find Margie's roots. September 2001**

*Ask where the good way is, and walk in it, and you will
find rest for your souls.* **Jeremiah 6:16**

Tracing My Roots

I was deeply absorbed in a book at Borders when my husband asked, "Is this what you have been looking for?" The map he put in front of me had a name in the southern end of the boot in Italy. Incredible! Tom had found Montaguto, the hilltop village of my ancestors!

For my 70th birthday, my family gave me a trip to Montaguto. We located relatives on both sides of my parentage and had a joyous time until September 11, 2001. It was 6:00 p.m. on the shore of Gallipoli, Italy, when a man rushed over to us and asked in broken English, "How far do you live from New York City?" After I told him he said, "Accidente! Accidente!" Before I could explain the conversation to Tom, the man rushed back to me and said, "No accidente! Terrorista!" We understood the crisis when we returned to the motel and saw the constant replay of the terror attacks on the Twin Towers. Air flights to the states were cancelled. I wondered if I would see my family again. Thankfully we returned to the states safely later that week.

As a child, the farthest I had traveled was to the Jersey shore. Tom and I traveled with our children to several states and Tom and I had been to Europe before 9/11. This was the most dramatic trip of my life.

Describe the travel you remember.

_____

_____

_____

_____

_____

_____

_____

_____

_____

_____

_____

Tell about a trip that gave you much pleasure.

_____

_____

_____

_____

_____

_____

_____

_____

_____

_____

_____

TURNING POINTS

This townhouse in Glen Mills, Pennsylvania became a turning point. The story is told in Buyer at the Door, in this chapter.

For I know the plans I have for you," declares the Lord, "plans to prosper you and not to harm you, plans to give you hope and a future." Jeremiah 29:11

How Much Does a Mother Cost?

Being a first grade teacher was an absolute joy for me. When my daughter was considering a career she told me that she thought about being a teacher because I always looked like I was having fun. She had been next door in a second grade class and used to come to my room at the end of the school day. Since she did not have to ride the bus, her teacher excused her early to come to my room.

Each day I lined up the children for lunch and asked each one to show me a bag lunch or the money to buy lunch. They knew that I would give them money to buy lunch if they had forgotten their lunch or money. One day, a child came to me and said, "Larry is not eating lunch these days." I said that Larry showed me lunch money every day. "Sure," said the boy, "but he is not eating. I sit next to him at the lunch table and I know that he doesn't eat!"

When the children returned to class I asked Larry what he was doing with his lunch money. He said. "I am saving up my money." "Does your mother know you are not eating?" "No," said Larry, "she's not home any more. That's why I'm saving the money. I want to buy a new mother. My mother went away. I want to buy you for my mother. I see how nice you treat kids, especially your daughter, when she comes to our class every day. I'm saving up. How much would it be to buy you for my mother?" "Larry," I said, "I am very sorry I cannot be your mother. We can have lunch together in my room every day and get to know each other better." "That's good!" said Larry. "I'll tell my grandmother about that. She is living with us now."

After school I told the principal and the nurse. The next day I invited Larry to have lunch with me at my desk while the class was in the lunch room. For the remaining two months of the year we had lunch together as we talked about school and his home life. I discovered that his mother had left for good because she did not want to be tied down. His father had not told the school staff because he decided it was none of their business.

I could not stop thinking of Larry all summer. That fall, I enrolled at a nearby university to get a Master's degree in counseling. It took me three years, going part time. I became a counselor. It was another career that was a match.

Something in Common

"Mom, you must meet my advisor," my daughter said. "I think you would really like him. You have a lot in common. You need to come now though. I am going to submit my open final and then the semester will end." My daughter Karen was at West Chester University getting a Master's degree in Counseling. I was still in North Brunswick and teaching at Rutgers University. Tom was working in Manhattan.

It was a clear spring day. Karen, her three year old Johnny, and I walked across campus to the advisor's office. Karen introduced us and Dr. Kahn asked what I was doing. "You should come here," he said. "We are currently interviewing for a position in your field."

"I would like to do that. I wish I lived closer to my children, but my husband works in New York City," I answered. "Speak to the department head anyway," he replied. I did. The department chair said, "You would have an extremely long commute!" True!

When my husband returned home from work that evening, he said, "I am thinking of retiring." I immediately updated my resume and mailed it to West Chester University. I was hired but my husband decided to work another several months. For almost a year, I did have an extremely long commute!

Buyer at the Door

"Maybe it is time to think about moving," I said. "Well," my husband answered, "we are happy in this townhouse. We moved near the children, as we wished. It is easy to care for."

"But these steps are getting to me. I would like a one floor house," I continued.

"Where would we go?" my husband asked. I had no answer. It was Labor Day, 2003. Just then there was a knock on the door. It was a friend of a neighbor.

"I want to buy your house," Al said. "I will give you the market price. You can take as long as you need to look for a home. I can move right in. You don't have to do a thing to your house." I could not believe what I heard. But I did hear it and exactly one year later we moved to a new community and a new lifestyle.

Describe a significant event in your life and how you handled the situation. The following are examples:

You are living alone after being married.
Your children have moved away from home.
An older relative has moved in with you.
You started a new job or developed a new hobby.

_____

_____

_____

_____

_____

_____

_____

_____

_____

_____

_____

_____

_____

_____

_____

_____

_____

_____

_____

_____

WORKING WORLD

Dr. Margaret Gibson in her office at West Chester University, where she served on the faculty until she retired in 1995.

Whatever you do, work at it with all your heart.
Colossians 3:23

A Nation in Transition

It was 1956, in the South. My husband, my 2 year old son, and I were making new friends in the apartment complex where we recently moved. The neighbors seemed friendly. Very few mothers worked outside the home then. One day I had a visitor. Actually, there were three visitors. Neighbors asked me to teach their children in my home.

The Civil Rights law was being tested. Integration was initiated in the local schools and these women refused to send their children to the local public school. After canvassing the apartment complex, they compiled a list of women who were stay at home moms and who were certified teachers. The list included me.

"You are just what we need," I was told. "We have secondary teachers in every subject but we need an elementary teacher. We will hold classes in our apartments. We will pay you."

I declined. "Why?" they asked. "I believe in integration," I said. The women were surprised. Although I felt very uncomfortable at that moment, I was grateful that these women, who had become my friends, remained my friends.

When have your values been tested either on your job or in your work as a volunteer?

_____

_____

_____

_____

_____

_____

_____

_____

_____

_____

_____

_____

_____

_____

_____

_____

_____

_____

_____

_____

_____

_____

_____

_____

It Isn't What Happens to You, It's What You Do About It

After I received a Master's degree in Counseling, I was hired at a local middle school. The first few weeks were filled with scheduling and orientation. No problem. Then, a school dance was announced. Viola was a student who had been confined to a wheel chair since birth. She and I ate lunch together in my office because she was not permitted to go outside. She accepted her restrictions cheerfully, until she found out about the dance.

"I wish I could go," Viola said, "but the principal will not let me." I encouraged her to have her mother intervene.

The day before the dance, Susan, another student, came to my office. The note from her teacher read, "Susan was taking a Social Studies test and got very upset. She insists on seeing you. She won't tell me why."

Susan told me that she awoke that morning and discovered a pimple on the end of her nose. "I can't go to the dance like this!" she wailed. "I can't concentrate on any test!" I suggested she ask her mother for make up. When I explained the consequences of not finishing the test she decided to go back to class. At noon, Viola came to my office. "Good news! I called my mom. She talked to the principal. I'm going to the dance!"

The following Monday I talked to both girls. Both had a great time. The make up worked for Susan and Viola showed me how she had twirled her wheel chair on the gym floor at the dance.

It was my first lesson as a counselor. Remember to help people realize that you may not have control over what happens to you. You do have control over what you do about it!

A small problem…or a big problem… How did you handle it?

_____

_____

_____

_____

Name two obstacles in your life and tell how you overcame them.

_____

_____

_____

_____

Who else was involved? Who helped you?

_____

_____

_____

_____

What did you learn about yourself from these problems?

_____

_____

_____

_____

What do you want people to remember about you?

_____

_____

_____

_____

_____

_____

_____

_____

_____

_____

_____

What legacy do you hope to leave?

_____

_____

_____

_____

_____

_____

_____

_____

_____

_____

_____

Show how unique you are. Complete the following sentences:

As a child I was

_____

_____

_____

Now I am

_____

_____

_____

My favorite thing to do on a rainy day is

_____

_____

_____

I am so glad I

_____

_____

_____

In the future I want to

_____

_____

A perfect day for me would be to

_____

_____

MEMORIES AND BEYOND

SHARING YOUR LEGACY

Album of photos with accompanying descriptions as explained in number three on the list below.

A good man leaves an inheritance for his children's children. **Proverbs 13:22**

1. Think of the house where you grew up. Attach a photo or drawing of it onto a frame. Write a memory about the house at the bottom of the photo. Place a photo of the house in an album. Write about experiences you had in that house.

2. Write a memory of a special occasion. Frame it and give it as a birthday gift to a family member or a friend.

3. Take photos around the house. Include objects with special meaning: paintings, vases, pillows, quilts, certificates. Put the photos in an album. Write a description of the photo on a 4'x 6 card o the opposite page.

4. Add dividers to a binder. Label the dividers according to highlights of your life (childhood, teen years, careers, vacations, parenting). Include letters, poems, and notes.

5. Create an album. for someone who was significant in your life (a parent, teacher, coach). Include communications and written memories.

6. Make an album of your favorites. Include your favorite colors, food, sports, and hobbies. Show the album to your children and other relatives. Encourage them to make albums of their favorites.

7. Turning Point Letters. Choose a person who influenced you when you made a big decision. If the person is living, write a thank you letter and mail it. If the person is deceased, write a memory of the person. Tell how that person influenced you.

8. Highlights of the Decades. Make a list of the stages of your life. Think of family, friends, school days, travels, and jobs. Choose an event from each decade of your life so far.

Childhood (up to 12 years of age)

_____

_____

_____

Teen years (13-19)

_____

_____

_____

As a Young Adult (20-40)

_____

_____

_____

The Middle Years (41-60)

_____

_____

_____

The Senior Years (61+)

_____

_____

_____

Frame this page and give it to a family member or friend as a birthday or anniversary gift.

EPILOGUE

**Celebrating the 50th anniversary of
Grandpop Tom and Grandmom Margie**

**Top row: Jeff, Tom, John
Second row down: Donna…Karen
Third row down: Brad, Greg, Margie,
First row, Jenny…Johnny**

**Margie and Tom welcome granddaughter Jenny's husband,
Jeff Lane, into the family June, 2009**

I thank my God every time I remember you. **Philippians 1:3**

The Needlework of Life

From the top of the mountain, I saw the small stone houses nestled in the trees. A 500 year old church was the only other building in the hilltop village. The visit to the land of my ancestors was a reminder of the millions of people who immigrated to America. The hardships in raising food on depleted land and life in a village with no heat or electricity brought me new admiration for those who toiled in the hilltop villages in Southern Italy.

What could I possibly bring back as a memento to my children and grandchildren? As I passed the open market, the aroma of fresh cheese and vegetables sweetened the air. It was not practical to return with food. Then, an elderly woman motioned to me. She was holding lace: large crocheted pieces with small stitched designs and tiny spaces in between. I asked if she had enough for my whole family. She answered, "There is always more."

When I arrived home I showed my daughter Karen some of the lace. She said, "What a wonderful way to show what life is. There are times when we feel sorrow and pain. They are the spaces in the lace. The spaces are surrounded by the beautiful needlework which shows the joy in our lives that we feel when we serve others and rejoice in God's goodness. Do you have more?" I smiled. "There is always more."

    E. E. Cummings wrote, *"It takes courage to grow up and become who you really are."*

BOOKS TO HELP YOU REMEMBER

The author's first book, *A Seed in Good Soil*, which details her childhood memories, gives Parenting Pointers, and helps readers recall their early lives.

The greatest use of a life is to spend it on something that will outlast it. **William James**

An American Childhood, Annie Dillard, Harper & Row, New York, NY, 1987

A Seed in Good Soil, Parenting Through Childhood Memories, Margaret Mayo Gibson, E-BookTime, LLC, Montgomery, Alabama, 2005

Eat, Pray, Love, Elizabeth Gilbert, Penguin Books, New York, NY, 2006

Family Treasures, Writing Your Life Stories, Margaret Mayo Gibson, E-BookTime, LLC, Montgomery, Alabama, 2009

Let Me Finish, Roger Angell, A Harvest Book, Harcourt, Inc. New York, NY, 2006

Look Me in the Eye, John Elder Robison, Crown Publishers, New York, NY, 2007

Marley and Me, John Grogan, HarperCollins, New York, NY, 2005

My Father's Secret War: A Memoir, Lucinda Franks, Hyperion Publishers, 2007

The Glass Castle, Jeannette Wall, Scribner, New York, NY, 2005

The Women Who Raised Me, Victoria Rowell, Harper Collins, New York, 2007

Turning Memories into Memoirs, Denis Ledoux, Soleil Press, Lisbon Falls, Maine, 1993

ABOUT THE AUTHOR

Margaret Mayo Gibson was born and raised in South Philadelphia. She was educated at the Philadelphia High School for Girls, Temple University, the College of New Jersey, and Rutgers University. Among Dr. Gibson's careers are Classroom Teacher, School Counselor, Child Development Specialist, Assistant Professor at Rutgers University and West Chester University, and Parenting Consultant.

Dr. Gibson is the author of parenting articles, devotionals, and the books, *A Seed in Good Soil*; *Parenting Through Childhood Memories*, and *Family Treasures, A Guide to Writing Your Life Stories*. Dr. Gibson and her husband, Thomas M. Gibson, live in Garnet Valley, PA, near their children and grandchildren.

Contact information and how to order:

A Seed in Good Soil, Parenting Through Childhood Memories, the author's first book, includes reminisces of the author's childhood in a parenting context and stimulates recall of life experiences.

Family Treasures, A Guide to Writing Your Life Stories, continues the author's life stories, then uses motivating questions to guide the reader in writing personal memories.

A Seed in Good Soil and *Family Treasures* may be ordered through the publisher at E-BookTime.com, through Amazon.com, or from the author at tgibowl@aol.com